℄ Creative Education

BY VALERIE BODDEN

Published by Creative Education
P.O. Box 227, Mankato, Minnesota 56002
Creative Education is an imprint of The Creative Company
www.thecreativecompany.us

Cover design and art direction by Rita Marshall
Interior design and book production by The Design Lab
Printed in the United States of America

Photographs by Alamy (Mary Evans Picture Library, John
Mitchell, North Wind Picture Archives, SouthAmerica
Photos, The London Art Archive, The Print Collector), The
Bridgeman Art Library (Eugene Deveria/Musee Bargoin/
Lauros/Giraudon), Corbis (Yann Arthus-Bertrand, Bettmann,
Christie's Images, Jim Erickson, North Carolina Museum of
Art, Greg Smith, The Art Archive), Getty Images (Newell
Convers Wyeth, English School, Kean Collection, Franco
Origlia, Spanish School)

Library of Congress Cataloging-in-Publication Data
Bodden, Valerie.
Columbus reaches the new world / by Valerie Bodden.
p. cm. – (Days of change)
Includes bibliographical references and index.
ISBN 978-1-58341-732-4
1. Columbus, Christopher–Travel–America–Juvenile literature.
2. America–Discovery and exploration–Spanish–Juvenile
literature. I. Title. II. Series.
E118.B63 2009
970.01'5–dc22   2008009163

First Edition
9 8 7 6 5 4 3 2 1

COLUMBUS REACHES THE NEW WORLD

The historic meeting of Christopher Columbus's crew and native islanders on October 12, 1492, was peaceful, although relations between the two cultures would later turn tragic.

Inquisitive islanders,

their naked bodies painted red, white, and black, peered at the sea, where three huge ships like none they had seen before towered above the water. Soon, smaller boats began to approach their island. When the boats reached the shore, men with white skin stepped from them and planted white flags decorated with green crosses in the sand. Curiously, the islanders approached the men. Although neither group could understand the other's language, goods were soon exchanged; the white men offered caps and beads, while the islanders brought parrots and thread.

This meeting on the morning of October 12, 1492, was the first significant encounter between the Old World of Europe, represented by Christopher Columbus and his men, and the New World of the Americas, represented by the Taino people of the Caribbean. Little did those gathered on the beach that morning know that their encounter would change the world. Soon, European settlers would flock to the Americas, bringing with them the products and culture of the Old World. They would also bring new diseases, which, along with slavery and violence, would kill 90 percent of the native population of the Americas, changing the face of the Western Hemisphere forever.

5

October 12, 1492

6

Columbus sailed to the Americas at a time when the different geographic regions of the world were marked by strikingly diverse cultures and civilizations. But these civilizations were beginning to communicate and trade with one another. Spices from Asia traveled to Europe by land, while building styles observed in the Middle East began to affect the architecture of India and several European countries. In the Americas, too, advanced civilizations traded both within and outside of their borders. Yet, the two halves of the world—the Eastern Hemisphere (Europe, Asia, and Africa) and the Western Hemisphere (the Americas)—had no knowledge of one another. Between them stretched some 3,000 miles (4,800 km) of ocean.

In the Americas, a population of 30 million to 100 million or more people was divided among hundreds of cultures. Each had its own religion, customs, language, and society. In the woodlands of northern and eastern North America lived the Iroquois and other groups that dwelt in longhouses (rectangular, bark-covered structures) or wigwams (bent or straight poles covered with bark or animal skins). They survived by hunting, fishing, and farming. The Cherokee and other people of the Southeast lived in villages along river valleys. And in the Southwest, groups of nomadic Apaches created terror as they raided the villages of neighboring tribes.

In Central and South America, numerous cultures also flourished. In Mexico, the vast Aztec empire, centered in Tenochtitlán (present-

TRADE AND TREASURE

Before Columbus's arrival, hundreds of different Indian tribes were strewn across the lands of North and South America, each celebrating its own unique customs and religions.

"*People have to realize that many Native Americans view America's worshiping Columbus as an insult. Even though the comparison may seem strange to some, many see him as a pre-colonial-day Hitler. He not only stripped Native Americans of their land, but their culture and livelihood.*"

WILMA MANKILLER,
first female chief of the
Cherokee Nation, 1991

day Mexico City), was at the height of its power in the late 1400s. Built on an island in the middle of the Lake of the Moon, Tenochtitlán was one of the largest cities in the world, with around 350,000 inhabitants. A large aqueduct system carried fresh water from the springs of the mainland onto the island, where spotless streets and boulevards crisscrossed the city. At the center of it all stood two pyramids to honor the gods. Farther south, in the Andes mountains of South America, the immense Inca empire was also thriving at the end of the 15th century. From its center in Cuzco (in present-day Peru), more than 25,000 miles (40,200 km) of roads connected the various regions of the empire. This advanced network of highways allowed for the easy transportation of animal hides and foods such as potatoes, beans, and peppers.

Today, North America is home to more than five million Native Americans, about half of whom live on reservations, or areas of land set aside for native peoples. Conditions on reservations are often grim, with high levels of poverty, although these areas are also centers of tribal culture. Other Native Americans live in cities throughout North America, with high concentrations in Chicago, Los Angeles, and Winnipeg, Manitoba. Meanwhile, Central and South America are home to a population of 40 to 49 million indigenous people today. The majority live in the Andes and the mountains of Central America, but many live in cities as well.

Machu Picchu, located in the Andes mountains of Peru, was once an Incan city that was home to some 1,000 members of the royal class, as well as important temples.

n Renaissance artists such as Leonardo da Vinci made elaborate studies of human omy and proportion, as in da Vinci's famous "Vitruvian Man," drawn around 1490.

Greek philosopher Plato

Meanwhile, across the world, the countries of Europe had embarked on a period in their history known as the Renaissance. Beginning in Italy in the 14th century and gradually spreading to other areas of Europe, the Renaissance was a cultural movement marked by a focus on the arts, sciences, and the classical learning of the Greeks and Romans. During this time period, great artists such as Italians Leonardo da Vinci and Michelangelo created masterfully realistic depictions of the human body, while scholars pored over the writings of the Greek philosopher Plato.

Throughout Europe, goods from the Far East were in high demand. Luxuries such as silk, precious stones, and porcelain, and spices such as pepper, cinnamon, and nutmeg made their way from Asia to homes across Europe. Despite this fact, most Europeans knew little about the "Indies," their name for all of eastern Asia from India to Japan. They were unaware, for example, that the people of China ate with chopsticks or that the emperor lived in an enormous, extravagant compound known as the Forbidden City, which commoners could not enter. They did know, however, that China was a land of untold wealth, based on the account of Venetian merchant Marco Polo, who had traveled to China (which he called Cathay) in the 13th century and written about its riches.

11

By the 15th century, however, land travel to the East was blocked by the Islamic Ottoman Empire, which was growing in strength and had conquered the city of Constantinople (present-day Istanbul, Turkey) in 1453. The Ottomans also controlled most trade with the East and charged the Europeans high prices for imported goods. As a result, the countries of Europe began to look for a new, sea-based route to the East. The invention of navigational aids such as the compass and the astrolabe (a tool for measuring the position of objects in the sky) and the construction of stronger ships meant that European explorers could sail the uncharted open ocean for the first time. Because Europeans' geographical knowledge was limited to their own continent, as well as small parts of Africa and Asia, these explorers sought not only to find a new route to the East

Constantinople's location at the juncture of Europe and Asia made it a rich and valuable city; it served for a time as a capital of the Roman Empire and, later, the Ottoman Empire.

In 1519, famed Portuguese explorer Ferdinand Magellan, working for Spain, set out to sail around the world. After crossing the Atlantic, rounding South America, and sailing across the Pacific Ocean, he arrived in the Indies. Although Magellan was killed there, his crew—which had been greatly reduced in number—sailed around Africa and returned to Spain. Nearly 400 years later, the Panama Canal was dug in Central America, cutting 9,000 miles (14,500 km) off the journey from one side of the world to the other. Today, more than 14,000 ships pass through the canal each year, carrying items such as automobiles, grain, and lumber between the Old World and the New.

FERDINAN. MAGALA.

This illustration of Ferdinand Magellan celebrates his famed voyage to the Indies, with monsters, storms, and fires representing the various dangers he faced and overcame.

but also to claim new lands. New lands meant new places to spread Christianity and to discover natural resources that would add wealth to their countries' treasuries.

Prince Henry the Navigator

With its long Atlantic coastline and many harbors, the tiny kingdom of Portugal became one of the first to sponsor overseas navigation. Beginning in the early 1400s, Prince Henry the Navigator sent numerous expeditions south along the coast of Africa. The expeditions were to search for a route around that continent to the Indian Ocean and the treasures of the East. As Portuguese ships traveled down the coastline of Africa, they found a continent ruled by rich and powerful kings who oversaw lands ranging in size from small villages to vast kingdoms. The Portuguese established trading posts along the African coast, where they exchanged horses, glass beads, bells, and carpets for African gold, ivory, and slaves.

At the same time that Portuguese sailors were attempting to sail around Africa, another explorer was developing his own plan to find a route to the East. Rather than traveling around Africa, however, Genoese-born Christopher Columbus wanted to sail west to the Indies across the Ocean Sea, as the Atlantic Ocean was then known. Because it was common knowledge by Columbus's time that Earth was a sphere, most

15

geographers agreed that travelers could get to the East by traveling west. What they didn't know was how much open ocean would have to be crossed before reaching the lands of Asia. After studying the works of ancient and contemporary geographers, Columbus concluded that the journey would be about 3,000 miles (4,800 km) long—short enough to be traversed without needing to stop and resupply. He also believed that Asia was a landmass that stretched so far north and south that explorers couldn't help but find it if they sailed far enough.

Armed with these beliefs and a determination to find a wealthy patron to sponsor his journey, Columbus approached King John II of Portugal to request royal backing. The king turned him down, however, as his royal advisers believed that the world was much larger than Columbus

During the late 1400s, Spain was busy trying to rid its land of non-Christians. Through the *Reconquista*, King Ferdinand and Queen Isabella hoped to "recapture" the kingdom of Granada, the last stronghold of the Islamic Moors who had taken over Spain in the 700s. In January 1492, they succeeded. At the same time, the Spanish Inquisition used torture against non-Christians who had insincerely converted to Christianity in order to escape persecution. In March 1492, the Spanish crown declared that all Jews had to either truly convert or leave the country by August 2—the day before Columbus embarked on his first voyage in search of the Indies.

Before he could take to the sea, Cristopher Columbus had to play the role of salesman, presenting
details of his intended voyage to European kings in hopes of obtaining royal sponsorship.

"*The whole history of the Americas stems from the four voyages of Columbus; and as the Greek city-states looked back to the deathless gods as their founders, so today a score of independent nations and dominions unite in homage to Christopher the stout-hearted son of Genoa.*"

Samuel Eliot Morison,
American historian, 1942

estimated. (They were right, as the distance westward from Europe to Asia is actually around 12,000 miles, or 19,300 km.) Undeterred, Columbus traveled to Spain and in 1486 presented his request to King Ferdinand II and Queen Isabella I. Busy overseeing a war against the Islamic Moors who ruled the southern Spanish land of Granada, the monarchs denied Columbus's request, although they said he could ask again at a later date.

Queen Isabella and King Ferdinand

In the meantime, Columbus sought support from Portugal again in 1488. This time, King John II denied the request because Portuguese explorer Bartolomeu Dias had just rounded the Cape of Good Hope at the southern tip of Africa. Thus, Portugal's hope of establishing a sea-based trade route with Asia was nearly realized, and Columbus's route was therefore not needed. Columbus also sought support from England, France, and possibly his home state of Genoa, Italy, all with no luck.

Then, after the Moors were defeated in January 1492, King Ferdinand II and Queen Isabella I of Spain finally agreed to sponsor Columbus. Within months, the elated Columbus headed to the Spanish port of Palos to make preparations for the journey westward. He had no idea that an entire, unknown continent stood in the way of his goal of reaching the Indies.

After seeking financial backing for more than seven years, Columbus finally secured the support he needed from Spain's monarchs, King Ferdinand II and Queen Isabella I.

Christopher Columbus set sail just before sunrise on the morning of August 3, 1492, with a fleet of three ships and a crew of around 90 men. Columbus himself sailed on the flagship, the *Santa María*, a broad, deep *não* ("ship" in Portuguese). Brothers Martín and Vicente Pinzón sailed the *Pinta* and the *Niña*, smaller vessels called caravels that were faster and more graceful than the *Santa María*. All three ships were stocked with enough fresh water, wine, salted meat, rice, beans, and other provisions to last a year. They also held trinkets such as glass beads, small copper bells, and woolen caps to be used in trade with the people of the Indies. In case their reception in the East wasn't completely friendly, the decks of the ships were mounted with cannons, and the men carried swords, crossbows, and muskets.

As the ships sailed into the open ocean, the men on board bid farewell to the Spanish coastline, which was out of sight by the second morning of the voyage. But the ships were not yet in uncharted territory, as Columbus made for Spain's Canary Islands off the northwest coast of Africa. In just under two weeks, the fleet arrived at the islands, where they waited for needed repair work to be completed on the *Pinta's* rudder. Finally, on September 6, the crew again took to the sea, this time unsure of when—or where—they would next see land.

Setting his course for due west, Columbus relied on the navigational art of dead reckoning to determine his position. By keeping careful track of his direction (based on compass readings) and speed (based on the length of time it took a piece of wood

20

The August 3rd departure of the *Santa María*, *Pinta*, and *Niña* was emotional; there was no telling how long the men on board would be gone, or if they would ever return to Spain.

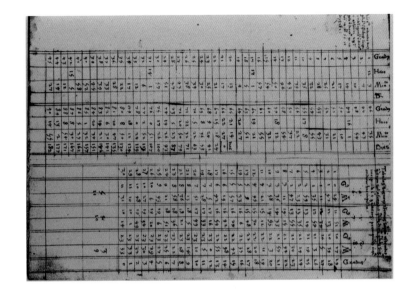

dropped in the water to pass from the ship's bow to its stern), Columbus could determine how far he had traveled. Because his crew members were not used to being so far from land, Columbus kept two records of the distance his fleet had covered. One figure represented the actual distance traveled, and the other was an underestimation. He reported the second figure to the men, so, as he wrote, "in case the voyage were long the men would not be frightened and lose courage."

As the ships continued to sail through the open water, the men settled into life at sea, working and resting in four-hour shifts. When they were not on duty, the sailors fished, gambled, or tried to sleep. Finding a comfortable spot to curl up for a nap wasn't easy, however, as the ships had no crew quarters (aside from small spaces for the officers). The men were forced to sleep on the bowed deck, exposed to the elements—although they

Columbus (shown opposite in his prime) consulted books on cosmography (above), some charts of which compared daylight hours at different latitudes, to help in his navigation of the sea.

"*At a very tender age, I went to sea sailing, and so I have continued to this day. The art of navigation leads the man who follows it to want to know the secrets of this world.*"

Columbus's fleet spent more than a month on the uncharted sea, enduring various trials that included bouts of heat, stretches of boredom, false sightings of land, and rough weather.

Christopher Columbus was born in Genoa, Italy, in 1451 and began to sail when he was a teenager. In 1476, a ship he was aboard sank off the coast of Portugal. After making his way back to shore by clinging to a floating oar, Columbus settled there, making his living as a chart maker and sailor. In 1479, Columbus married Felipa Moniz Perestrello, and the two had a son, Diego. Six years later, following his wife's death, Columbus moved to Spain. He later met Beatriz Enriquez de Harana, with whom he had another son, Ferdinand. According to Ferdinand, Columbus was "pleasant, although grave and dignified."

crowded into the cargo space below deck during the worst weather.

Just over a week after leaving the Canaries, on September 14, the men spotted two birds, which Columbus said was a sign that land was near. Two days later, the ships came upon an area of the ocean covered with sargassum, a floating plant that Columbus mistakenly believed had been ripped from rocks on shore. The captain reminded his men to be on the lookout for land. He even offered a new coat and 10 months' wages to the man who first spotted it. On September 25, Martín Pinzón, captain of the *Pinta*, claimed the reward, saying he had seen land to the southwest. As the ships sailed on, however, it became clear that the "land" he had seen had been squall clouds.

After another false sighting of land on October 7, the crew became restless, and by October 10, mutiny seemed close at hand. Columbus was aware of his crew's discontent but was determined to push on. He wrote in his log, "[The men] grumbled and complained of the long voyage, and I reproached them for their lack of spirit. . . . I also told the men that it was useless to complain, for I had started out to find the Indies and would continue until I had accomplished that mission." Yet, to appease his crew, Columbus agreed that if they hadn't spotted land within three days, they would turn back.

The next night, as he peered out over the dark waters, Columbus thought he saw a light in the distance. A few hours later, early in the morning of October 12, a crewman aboard the *Pinta* called "*Tierra*! *Tierra*!" After 3,200 miles (5,150 km) and 33 days at sea, land had been spotted at last.

When daylight revealed the shoreline of an island, Columbus ordered the ships anchored. Then he, the Pinzón brothers, fleet secretary Rodrigo de Escobedo, and comptroller (financial officer) Rodrigo Sanchez made their way to shore in the fleet's launches. As curious natives looked on, Columbus planted the flags of the Spanish crown in the sand, then knelt and offered a prayer of thanks to God. Afterward, he stood up and ordered the men with him to bear witness that he

"Columbus's first journey took just thirty-three days, but it was to change the outlook of the world forever. His explorations in 1492 led mankind on a path of discovery that has never ceased to challenge and surprise us. As a result of this man's great courage and determination, ideas and people have passed between the Old World and the New World for half a millennium. Christopher Columbus not only opened the door to a New World, but also set an example for us all by showing what monumental feats can be accomplished through perseverance and faith."

U.S. PRESIDENT GEORGE
H. W. BUSH, 1989

26

Five centuries after Columbus arrived in the Bahamas, historians still debate which island in the chain was the location of the explorer's first landfall in the Americas. In the last 150 years, at least nine different islands have been proposed. The two most likely contenders are Watling Island and Samana Cay, located only 60 miles (96.5 km) from one another. In 1926, Watling was renamed San Salvador by British officials (Britain possessed the island at the time). Although they used the name Columbus had given to the island of landfall as testament to their belief that this was the first island discovered, the debate continues.

The region in which Columbus made landfall—the Bahamas—includes hundreds of islands, making it unlikely historians will ever know for certain where Columbus first set foot.

This illustration captures the scene of Columbus's New World arrival: weary crewmen with weapons and a clergyman with a crucifix give thanks to God for their landfall.

Much of what we know about Columbus's first voyage comes from his log, in which he kept a careful record of his ships' progress. He also wrote about the beauty of the Americas, with descriptions such as, "The song of the little birds might make a man wish never to leave here." When he returned to Spain, Columbus presented his log to Queen Isabella I, who had it copied. Unfortunately, both the original and the copy were eventually lost. But a summary of the log written by Bartolomé de Las Casas, a friend of the Columbus family, survives today. The summary includes many of Columbus's exact words.

was "taking possession of this island for the King and Queen." He gave the island the name San Salvador ("Holy Savior" in Spanish).

Although Columbus thought that the land he was claiming for Spain was in Asia, he was actually in the Bahamas, a chain of islands in the Caribbean Sea southeast of present-day Florida. The island he had landed on was called Guanahani by its inhabitants, the Taino people. These people were tall and tan, with wide, flat foreheads (from their custom of binding the heads of children) and straight, coarse hair. Almost immediately, Columbus noted that the Tainos were incredibly friendly, writing in his log that they "became so much our friends that it was a marvel. . . . They took everything [we gave them] and gave of what they had very willingly."

After only two days on San Salvador, Columbus decided to begin his quest for gold, and, taking six Tainos on board to serve as guides, he and his crew sailed on to explore the nearby islands. As he traveled, Columbus noted the beauty of the land, whose trees were "as different from ours as day is from night," and the fragrance of the flowers that could be smelled even from the sea.

On a large island that came to be known as Hispaniola, Columbus and his men found large Taino villages, some home to up to 2,000 people. Most of the homes in the villages were round, constructed of thatch and wooden posts, and sheltered several related families. The Tainos lived largely by farming yams, corn, potatoes, and peppers, and by fishing. They were skilled in making pottery, weaving cotton, and carving, and fashioned nuggets of gold into ornaments for their pierced noses. Although Columbus and his men

In 1503, Columbus found himself exploring the Caribbean with two ships that were no longer seaworthy. Shipworms, or long, wood-eating mollusks, had bored so many holes into the ships that Columbus had to beach the vessels on the island of Jamaica. A handful of crew members and Tainos departed in canoes to request help from Hispaniola. Because of conflicts with Nicolás de Ovando, the new governor of Hispaniola, though, the men couldn't return with help for almost a year. In the meantime, Columbus and the 100 or so sailors left in Jamaica survived only by the generosity of the Tainos, who supplied them with food.

In the two cultures' early interactions, the Tainos were impressed by the whites' metals and fine attire, and the Spaniards were impressed by the natives' friendly curiosity.

Although it is known the 70-foot (21 m) *Santa María* (shown here wrecking) was made of oak and pine, the ship's exact structuring was never recorded and remains unknown.

were excited to see this gold jewelry, they were disappointed to learn that the Tainos had little other gold to trade with them. Still, relations between the two groups remained mostly positive, although indications that this would not always be the case could already be seen in Columbus's logbook entry that the Tainos would make "good and intelligent servants."

Columbus's explorations of the islands came to an abrupt end in the early morning of December 25, 1492, when the *Santa María*, under the command of a less experienced seaman, ran aground on a coral reef off the coast of Hispaniola. Although all of the men were able to get safely off the vessel, Columbus was devastated by the loss of his flagship. He ordered that a fort be constructed on the island from the ship's remains. Naming the fort Navidad, Columbus stationed 39 of his men there, and in early January 1493, he and the rest of his crew headed back to Spain aboard the *Niña* and the *Pinta*. They left behind a land that had already been changed forever by their presence.

> *"It was a miracle that these wonderful lands had remained unknown to the rest of the world through all history, and were saved by God to be discovered in our time."*
>
> PEDRO CIEZA DE LEON,
> Spanish conquistador, 1550s

33

When he arrived back in Spain, Columbus was hailed as a hero. People across the country were amazed by what he had brought back with him: exotic flowers, gold jewels, brightly colored parrots, and six Tainos wearing feathers and fish-bone ornaments.

King Ferdinand II and Queen Isabella I were impressed, too. The monarchs honored Columbus with the title "Admiral of the Ocean Sea" and made him viceroy and governor of the islands he had discovered. They also asked him to prepare immediately for a second trip—this time to colonize the new land. On September 25, 1493, Columbus set sail for Hispaniola with a fleet of 17 vessels and more than 1,000 men, including his brother Diego. When the men arrived, though, they discovered that the fort of Navidad had been destroyed. All of the men were dead, killed by one another and by a group of Tainos they had mistreated. After establishing a new settlement called Isabela, Columbus left Diego in charge and set sail for Cuba, which he believed was the Asian mainland.

When the admiral returned to Hispaniola from his explorations in September 1494, he found the island in disorder. Many of the Spaniards there had raided Taino villages and stolen the Indians' food. In desperation, the Tainos now attempted to fight back, but they were no match for the Spaniards' crossbows and guns. Thousands of Tainos were taken captive.

Soon, Columbus found a new use for them. Because he needed to

THE NEW FACE OF THE NEW WORLD

Columbus's triumphant return to Spain was cause for much celebration, and the tales he brought back—along with Tainos and New World animals and fruits—made him a hero.

"*Everything that has happened since the . . . discovery of the Americas has been so extraordinary that the whole story remains quite incredible to anyone who has not experienced it at first hand. . . . It seems to . . . silence all talk of other wonders of the world.*"

BARTOLOMÉ DE LAS CASAS,
Spanish priest, 1542

Although the Taino culture has disappeared from the world, the people Columbus first came into contact with in the New World have made their presence felt in the English language. The Taino had no written language, but the Spaniards wrote down the Taino words for various objects. Words such as barbecue, canoe, hurricane, iguana, maize, and manatee all have their origin in the Taino language. From the Taino, we also get the word tobacco, a plant that the Europeans first came into contact with in the New World. The Taino also introduced the Spaniards to both the word hammock and the object's use.

The Taino people worshiped two supreme gods—Yúcahu and Ababey—as well as various lesser gods, which were sometimes represented in carvings or rock petroglyphs.

repay the Spanish monarchs for funding his trip but had found little gold with which to do so, Columbus decided to turn to another financial resource: human merchandise. In February 1495, he ordered 500 of the Taino captives to be sent to Spain as slaves. About 200 Tainos died during the voyage, however, and the rest were so weakened from the journey that they died soon afterward.

Even while many of their fellow villagers from Hispaniola were being shipped overseas to serve as slaves, thousands of other Tainos on the island found themselves enslaved at home. By 1496, the Spaniards had forcibly taken over all of Hispaniola, and, as governor, Columbus imposed a gold tax on the natives. Every three months, each Taino 14 years or older had to provide a small bell full of gold (amounting to about half an ounce, or 14 g) to the Spaniards. Because there were no large deposits of gold on the island, the natives were forced to sift gold dust from the sand and streams. Often, those who could not come up with the required amount had a hand chopped off.

After setting up such a brutal system, Columbus ordered his recently arrived brother Bartholomew to construct a new capital called Santo Domingo on Hispaniola. Then, in March

"Must we celebrate another Columbus Day? . . . Columbus was merely the first conqueror of a 'New World' ruled by Native Americans for 3,000 years. He introduced slavery, exploitation, and death to the most populated part of the globe. . . . What we need is a holiday to celebrate the upwards of 75 million people who lived here in peace in 1492 and then mounted a resistance."

WILLIAM LOREN KATZ, historian and professor at New York University, 2003

37

1496, the admiral returned to Spain. He remained there until May 1498, when he embarked on his third voyage for what was still thought to be the Indies. After briefly touring the coast of South America, which Columbus believed was a continent south of China, the admiral returned to Santo Domingo. There, he found trouble. Faced with food shortages and a lack of gold, a large group of colonists had revolted against his rule. Soon, complaints that the Columbus brothers were poor governors who were unable to maintain control and often resorted to harsh punishments reached the Spanish crown. In 1500, judge Francisco de Bobadilla was sent to investigate. What he found—seven Spaniards hanging from a gallows for rebellion—led him to arrest Columbus and his brothers and send them back to Spain in chains.

Some people today take exception to the idea that Christopher Columbus "discovered" America. Some say that the Native Americans already knew that the land was here, so Columbus didn't discover anything at all. Others point out that a Viking explorer named Leif Ericson arrived in the Americas around the year 1000. Although accounts of Ericson's voyage differ, it appears that he settled in Newfoundland or Nova Scotia, Canada, for a short time before abandoning the harsh landscape and unfriendly natives. Because news of Ericson's voyage never spread, it made little impact in Europe and was all but forgotten by Columbus's time.

Within three years of Columbus's arrival in the New World, the Spaniards—hungry for wealth—were plundering native villages in order to obtain gold and slave labor.

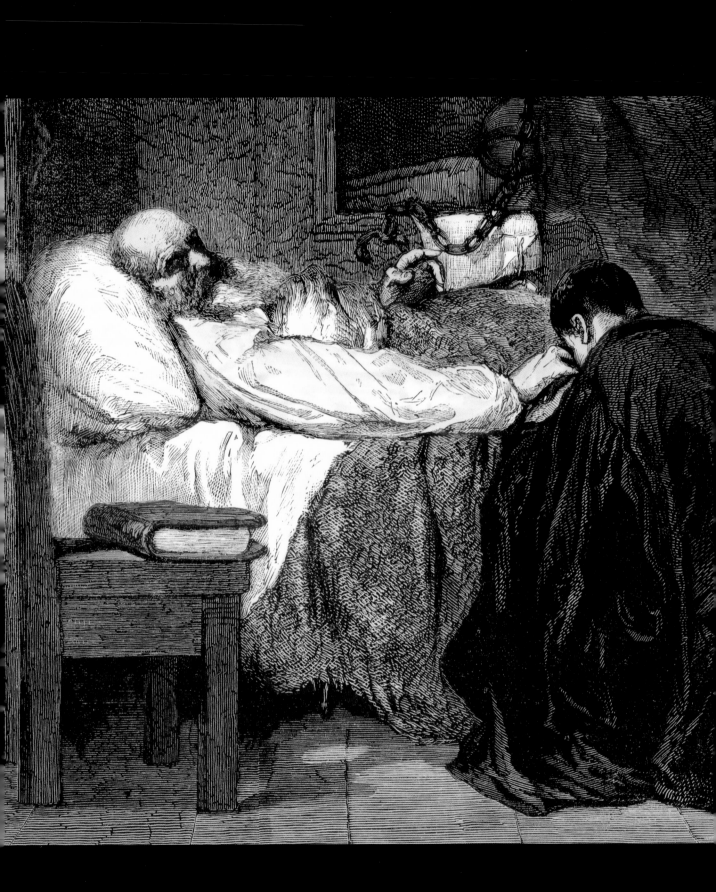

At the time of his death in 1506, Columbus was at odds with the Spanish crown; he demanded 10 percent of all profits made in the New World, but the monarchy rejected it.

Because Columbus never realized that the lands he had sailed to were not part of the Indies, but were rather a new continent, that continent was not named after him. Instead, the Americas take their name from Amerigo Vespucci, an explorer from Florence, Italy. Vespucci traveled to South America twice between 1499 and 1502 and wrote in a letter that the lands should be called a "New World, because our ancestors had no knowledge of them." His letter was widely publicized, and in 1507, the Latinized version of his name—"America"—first appeared on a map of the world.

Although Ferdinand and Isabella immediately pardoned Columbus, his position as governor of the islands was stripped from him. Yet, he was allowed to make one more voyage there in May 1502. This time, Columbus explored the coast of Central America and spent time marooned on Jamaica before heading back to Spain in November 1504. Two years later, on May 20, 1506, the Admiral of the Ocean Sea died.

Although Columbus insisted to his dying day that he had found a new route to Asia, by the early 1500s, some geographers had begun to suspect that he had actually sailed to a previously unknown continent in a new part of the world. This "New World" was given the name America in 1507. Settlers from Spain continued to flock there, and by 1508, there were 8,000 to 10,000 Spaniards on Hispaniola. Soon they were forming settlements on the other islands of the Caribbean as well. The result of such a huge influx of Europeans to their world was devastating to the Tainos, many of whom died of overwork as they continued to be forced into slavery.

As devastating as slavery was, the biggest cause of death for the Caribbean natives after the arrival of the Europeans wasn't servitude, but disease. In 1493, the first smallpox outbreak hit Hispaniola, and soon, other diseases such as measles, whooping cough, and cholera were killing off huge numbers of natives, who had no immunity to these Old World illnesses. By 1548, fewer than 500 Tainos remained of the 300,000 to 1 million who had lived on Hispaniola when Columbus first arrived. The population of the Guanahatabeys and Island-Caribs, smaller native groups in the Caribbean, also declined.

The natives of the Caribbean islands weren't the only ones to suffer from the arrival of the Europeans, however. Throughout the 16th century, Spanish explorers called *conquistadores* voyaged to the Central and South American mainland, discovering and conquering native societies, including the Aztecs and Incas. The natives of North America didn't fare as badly at first, as European colonization of their continent didn't occur in ear-

"Your greed for gold is blind. Your pride, your lust, your anger, your envy, your sloth, all blind. . . . For you are destroying an innocent people. . . . By what right do you make them die? Mining gold for you in your mines or working for you in your fields, by what right do you unleash enslaving wars upon them? They lived in peace in this land before you came, in peace in their own homes. They did nothing to harm you to cause you to slaughter them wholesale."

FRAY ANTÓN MONTECINO, Spanish priest in Santo Domingo, in a 1510 sermon to Spanish colonists

New World natives were decimated by Old World diseases; after smallpox appeared on islands such as Hispaniola, it plagued Central and North America for more than 200 years.

nest until the 17th century. Still, by the end of the 16th century, as many as 90 percent of the natives of the Americas—possibly up to 90 million people—were dead.

As they explored and conquered the Americas, the Spanish plundered the silver and gold of the New World. They sent the precious metals back to their homeland, which soon became the most powerful country in Europe. Along with gold and silver, New World crops such as potatoes, corn, and peanuts were also carried to the Old World. At the same time, new animals such as horses and cattle and new crops such as rice and bananas were introduced to the Americas. This exchange of products between the Eastern and Western Hemispheres came to be known as the Columbian Exchange.

The Columbian Exchange was also responsible for bringing a new culture to the New World, as the Spanish introduced European art, city planning, architecture, and the Christian religion to the Americas. In addition, the first Spanish settlers to the region began the formation of a new group of people in Latin America (the part of the Western Hemisphere south of the present-day United States). Because Spanish women were rare in the first American settlements, Spanish men often took native wives. Their children, known as *mestizos*, represented a blend of native and Spanish cultures.

"Many persons mocked the Admiral for the enterprise he wanted to carry out, going to discover the Indies. . . . And they taunted the Admiral in public and considered his enterprise foolish, which thing he heard said in public by many persons in this city [Palos, Spain] and outside."

JUAN RODRIGO CABEZUDO, resident of a town near Palos, 1520s

44

Although Spanish explorers first approached cultures such as the Incas with teachings of Christianity, they soon used their horses and advanced weaponry to conquer the natives.

Columbus Day is widely observed today, even in countries such as Peru, where Spaniards once overran and transformed local cultures to serve the interests of their distant homeland.

Today, the mestizo culture is celebrated in many parts of Latin America on *Día de la Raza*, or Day of the Race. This holiday is observed each October 12 (the anniversary of Columbus's first arrival in the Americas) with parades and other festivities. In the U.S., Columbus's landing in the Americas has been commemorated as Columbus Day since 1937. Yet not everyone celebrates Columbus's arrival in the New World. Throughout the Americas, many native peoples despise Columbus. They say that he invaded their land and instituted a system of conquest, slavery, and exploitation. Whether people today view Columbus's arrival in the Americas as one of the best or one of the worst events in the history of the world, it was certainly one of the most momentous, changing forever the lives of all who would come after him in both the New World and the Old.

"The first footfall of Columbus on the shore of the New World echoed like a thunderclap down the centuries, and its reverberations have not yet died away."

LUIS MARDEN, American explorer, photographer, and writer, 1992

47

The Christian religion and the Spanish language illustrate Spain's influence on Central and South America even today, more than 500 years after Columbus's arrival.

BIBLIOGRAPHY

Columbus, Christopher. *The Log of Christopher Columbus*. tr. by Robert Fuson. Camden, Maine: International Marine Publishing, 1992.

Dor-Ner, Zvi. *Columbus and the Age of Discovery*. New York: William Morrow, 1991.

Heat-Moon, William Least. *Columbus in the Americas*. Hoboken, N.J.: John Wiley & Sons, 2002.

Jacobs, Francine. *The Tainos: The People Who Welcomed Columbus*. New York: G. P. Putnam's Sons, 1992.

Pelta, Kathy. *Discovering Christopher Columbus: How History Is Invented*. Minneapolis: Lerner, 1991.

Rouse, Irving. *The Tainos: Rise & Decline of the People Who Greeted Columbus*. New Haven, Conn.: Yale University Press, 1992.

Stannard, David. *American Holocaust: Columbus and the Conquest of the New World*. New York: Oxford University Press, 1992.

INDEX

Africa 6, 12, 14, 15, 19, 20
American Indians 6, 8, 9, 26, 29, 30, 33, 34, 36, 37, 39, 42, 44, 47
  Aztecs 6, 8, 42
  Incas 8, 42
  Tainos 5, 29, 30, 33, 34, 36, 37, 42
    enslavement of 5, 34, 37, 42
    trade with 5, 33
Canary Islands 20, 25
Caribbean islands 27, 29, 30, 33, 34, 37, 38, 41, 42
  Hispaniola 30, 33, 34, 37, 38, 41, 42
    Santo Domingo 37, 38
  Jamaica 30, 41
  San Salvador 27, 29
Central America 6, 9, 14, 41, 42
Christianity 15, 16, 44
Columbian Exchange 44
Columbus, Christopher
  arrest 38
  death 41
  family 25, 34, 37
  first voyage 5, 16, 19, 20, 22, 25, 26, 27, 29, 30, 33
    distance 16, 19, 22, 26
    landfall 5, 26, 27, 29
    navigation 20, 22, 23

  fourth voyage 41
  log 26, 29, 33
  search for gold 30, 33, 37
  second voyage 34, 36, 37
  third voyage 38
Columbus Day 37, 47
conquistadores 33, 42
diseases 5, 42
Indies (eastern Asia) 11, 12, 14, 15, 16, 19, 20, 26, 29, 38, 41, 44
  trade routes to 11, 12, 14, 15, 16, 19
Italy 11, 19, 25, 41
Magellan, Ferdinand 14
mestizos 44, 47
Niña 20, 33
Pinta 20, 25, 26, 33
Pinzón, Martín 20, 25, 26
Pinzón, Vicente 20, 26
Polo, Marco 11
Portugal 15, 16, 19, 25
Santa María 20, 33
South America 6, 8, 9, 14, 38, 41, 42
Spain 14, 16, 19, 20, 25, 26, 29, 33, 34, 37, 38, 41, 44
  King Ferdinand II 16, 19, 34, 38
  Queen Isabella I 16, 19, 29, 34, 38
Vespucci, Amerigo 41